Horace Stillman

The Poetic Story of the Hero of the Ocean

Or, Christopher Columbus from his birth to life's crowning

achievement-The discovery of America

Horace Stillman

The Poetic Story of the Hero of the Ocean
*Or, Christopher Columbus from his birth to life's crowning achievement-The
discovery of America*

ISBN/EAN: 9783337037833

Printed in Europe, USA, Canada, Australia, Japan

Cover: Foto ©ninafisch / pixelio.de

More available books at **www.hansebooks.com**

THE POETIC STORY

OF THE HERO OF THE OCEAN

OR

CHRISTOPHER COLUMBUS FROM HIS BIRTH
TO LIFE'S CROWNING ACHIEVEMENT—
THE DISCOVERY OF AMERICA

BY

Rev. HORACE STILLMAN, A.M.

1893

PREFACE.

ATTENTION, reader ! while I tell
The story that is known so well—
The story old, the story true,
Here dressed in verbal vesture new,
Of how Columbus saw the light,
In a dark age of error's night,
That wisdom's sons had never found,
By which he proved "this world is round."
How that illustrious hero bold
Then faced the frowns of young and old,
And stormy winds both loud and frantic,
Until he crossed the wild Atlantic,
And found and gave the world the key
To this dear land of liberty.

THE AUTHOR.

CONTENTS.

CHAPTER I.

CHAPTER II.

CHAPTER III.

CHAPTER IV.

CHAPTER V.

CHAPTER VI.

CHAPTER VII.

CHAPTER VIII.

CHAPTER IX.

CHAPTER X.

CHAPTER XI.

CHAPTER XII.

CHAPTER XIII.

CHAPTER XIV.

QUEEN ISABELLA.

THE POETIC STORY OF THE HERO OF THE OCEAN.

CHAPTER I.

BESIDE a lovely mountain,
  On a fair Italian shore,
Stands in her pride of glory
  The city of Genoa.

Lost in the mists of ages
  Is the record of her birth,
But she gave to fame immortal
  One whose praise now fills the earth.

Born was he of humble parents
  Having but a common name,
Toiling daily for life's comforts,
  Dreaming not of wealth or fame.

But this son had to him given
    Eyes to see and ears to hear,
A brave, commanding, noble spirit,
    Yielding not to idle fear.

To the famous school of Pavia,
    There our destined hero went,
And in cosmographic study
    All his energies were bent.

Here he thought beyond his teaching,
    And an added truth soon found—
That this earth, so broad and massive,
    Was not flat, but nearly round.

That, beyond the rolling waters
    Of the ever restless sea,
Other land not yet discovered
    He was certain there must be.

Now he sails the Mediterranean
    For the benefit of trade,
And there in little open vessels
    Many trips so safely made.

Then he passed the shores of Iceland.
    To explore a northern route,
Where a century before
    Other vessels were sent out.

Then he sailed the southern waters,
    Passing Guinea's verdant shore,
As far he went as any vessel
    Ever there had been before.

Now he goes to famous Lisbon,
  Where there lived a daring band,
Famous for their explorations,
  Looking for some unknown land.

Here he thought and planned and studied,
  Living now a quiet life,
And here he won a Miss Felipa—
  A fair Italian—for his wife.

Here was born his son Diego,
  Lad of promise bright and fair,
Soon to pass beneath the shadows,
  And his father's loss to share.

In thought Columbus roamed the waters
  While giving still his hand to art,
Making for his fellow sailors
  Old Ocean's latest map and chart.

While awake, he thought and pondered
  Of a distant unknown shore,
Where he hoped to be directed
  By the God that we adore.

In his dreams he sailed and landed,
  Meeting not a serious loss,
Where at last he proudly planted
  The sacred banner of the cross.

Through this hope his soul was lighted ;
  By this, all danger he could meet ;
He would cross the pathless ocean,
  Could he only get a fleet.

He would man an expedition,
  Had he wealth at his command,
That would sail the western waters
  Till they reach fair India's land.

Could he get the needed treasures,
  And his hopes to practice bring?
What would be the royal dictum
  Should he stand before the king?

Moved to act by these reflections,
  Like a bird upon the wing,
He hastens to King John, at Lisbon,
  His plans to lay before the king.

CHAPTER II.

COLUMBUS BEFORE KING JOHN THE SECOND AND HIS COUNCIL.

Soon he tells the listening monarch
  That this world is nearly round,
And beyond old ocean's waters
  Other land could yet be found.

Asks of him his kind assistance,
  An expedition to command,
That he might make an exploration,
  Seek and find the distant land.

Tells him how 'twould help his nation,
  Wealth and honor to it bring,
That it might extend his kingdom,
  How 'twould help his honored king.

To these words the king responded :
  . " You may think the world is round,
But I'm not prepared to tell you
  That your views in this are sound,

" That there is land beyond the ocean,
  This you surely do not know ;
Should I raise an expedition,
  To destruction it might go.

" This is not the ultimatum ;
  I will give decision when
All your plans have been submitted
  To my scientific men."

So with the king he meets that council,
  Where the wisest ones are found,
Tells them one by one the reasons
  Why he thinks the world is round.

Were it flat way in the distance,
  O'er the land or waters wide,
It must have a termination,
  When you reach the outer side,

Like a pit without a bottom,
  Reaching all the world around,
Where the heedless, headlong falling,
  Could never be by mortals found ;

Where a vessel thither sailing
  Makes a fearful downward lunge,
Ever falling, rolling, sinking,
  In her dreadful, fatal plunge.

Ocean could not hold its waters,
  Its banks would tumble day by day ;
Then in rolling, rushing torrents
  Would quickly pour itself away.

Other proofs he laid before them,
  Other reasons, mainly sound ;
Giving facts that were substantial
  Why he thought the world was round.

If the earth is round or oval,
  Then why need one's efforts fail,
Should he boldly launch upon it,
  And attempt around to sail?

From east to west the Mediterranean
  Two thousand miles he knew to be;
He found the time the sun was passing
  O'er this measured inland sea.

The sunshine measuring thus its way
Goes clear around the earth each day;
Now by proportion can be found
The distance all the world around.

That there are unknown lands at sea
Is very evident to me;
For on an island, an Azore,
Two human bodies washed ashore,

And in their forms was found no trace
Of any now known human race;
Wood has also washed ashore
Unlike any known before.

Carvings thus have reached these lands,
Rudely cut by unskilled hands;
Cut by implements obtuse,   ·
Unlike any known in use.

As he had told the king before,
He tells them how to reach that shore,
And what advantage it would be
To find a way across the sea.

His schemes before them now were laid ;
To him this answer then they made :
Can any such a fool be found
Who really thinks the world is round ?

Man on the downward side, they said,
Would have his heels above his head ;
All in country and in town,
Inverted thus must walk around.

And here must everyone you meet
Have shoes adhesive on his feet.
How far, then, could any go,
Before they headlong fell below ?

So everything, as all must see,
Would surely topsy-turvy be ;
Trees would grow with branches down,
While the roots above were in the ground.

The rain and hail and fleecy snow
Must upwards fall from depths below ;
The birds that wing the azure sky,
All upon their backs would fly.

Should a ship at your command
Sail and reach a distant land,
. Down, far down, this round, steep track
No power on earth could get it back.

Why need this council answer more,
Concerning what has washed ashore ?
What of the measured distance found ?
The world, you see, cannot be round.

To close, what must the answer be,
From us, the learnèd Portugue'?
Should such an expedition go ?
We most respectfully answer, no !

CHAPTER III.

THOUGH they dismissed him with a jeer,
His words burn in that sovereign's ear.
Such earnest words! so strange and new!
But may they not, indeed, be true?

That he may of a certain know,
He'll have an expedition go;
In secret he will fit it out,
And have it follow close the route,

That so clear Columbus made
While he before the council staid.
If other lands were found at sea,
The credit to himself would be.

So now he turns from this appeal,
His thoughts and plans to meanly steal.
Men knew not what he was about
When soon he sent a vessel out.

For it appeared, when it went,
To Cape Verde Island to be sent;
But to its captain he had said,
" Now boldly push your boat ahead;

" Follow first the well-known track,
But do not bring your vessel back
Until your feet shall surely stand
Upon the distant unknown land."

The vessel sailed, and passed that shore
That so well was known before ;
But when she headed out to sea,
Where not a harbor there could be,

The crew were filled with fear and dread ;
And every league she pushed ahead,
Receding farther from the shore,
Their fears were quickened more and more.

While in this mood of discontent
A storm old ocean's bosom rent.
A grand, terrific, sweeping gale
Madly struck their quivering sail.

The waves rolled high, the white caps pranced,
The vessel on the billows danced ;
Dark forebodings added came,
Until they cursed that captain's name.

Why should he bring them here to die,
Beneath the cold dark sea to lie?
For all the world they would not be
So tossed upon that raging sea.

Above the roaring sea they shout,
" Let's head the vessel right about !
O captain, captain, we implore,
Speed us most quickly back to shore ! "

"No! Let the vessel go ahead!"
In anger then the captain said.
" For such a raging, howling blast
Will soon pass by! It cannot last."

But the vessel tossed and swayed,
Plunge after plunge she quickly made.
Oh what terror! Oh what dread!
As one was pitched upon his head.

Others reeling, staggering go,
Or creeping on their knees, below.
" For mercy sake!" again they shout,
" You bring at once this ship about!

" If you propose to onward go,
We'll send you to the depths below!"
When thus persuasively appealed,
The captain thought it best to yield.

"I cannot blame you, men," he said,
" That such a storm should cause you dread;
We'll go no farther on this route,
So let the vessel go about.

" Let her, now, carry all her sail,
And quickly fly before the gale."
And so they sped at his command,
Until they reached their native land.

Now when the captain and the crew
Around their king in caution drew,
And as they there before him stand
They disbelieve in unknown land.

Dark were the plans the king had lain
That he might wealth and honor gain ;
But all the honor stealth can bring
Is very quickly on the wing.

Instead of writing high his name
On lofty monument of fame,
His tarnished name was written low
Where everyone could see and know.

CHAPTER IV.

COLUMBUS LEAVES IN DISGUST FOR GENOA.

Now when this perfidy so mean
Was by Columbus plainly seen,
That such a " great and honored king "
Should now this stain upon him bring,

He cared of him to know no more,
And started soon for old Genoa,
Hoping a better chance to stand
In his own dear native land.

Before the Genoese he laid
All the schemes that he had made ;
But they were called at once erratic,
The visions of a great fanatic.

Has not old Lisbon's council set,
And all of these delusions met ?
The wisest of the world there came,
Above all other men in fame.

Who is this man ? Do you not know
That on the throne of kings would go
Domenico Colombo's son,
Who never any glory won ?

A fellow of the poorest sort,
A sailor from this very port ;
His father now, does he not still
Live over there beside the hill ?

He never had his coffer full
Unless he filled it combing wool ;
A wiser man this son had made
Had he but learned his father's trade.

And so this man of humble birth
Was made the butt of scorn and mirth.
He need not dream to gain renown
In his own home, his native town.

Such was his doom.   It seemed that fate
Had caused this anxious soul to wait
Till from the furnace he could bear
All of the woes that he must share.

CHAPTER V.

COLUMBUS GOES TO SPAIN AND SEEKS ASSISTANCE FROM QUEEN
ISABELLA.

WHAT here at home he sought in vain,
He now resolves to find in Spain.
Will Ferdinand and Isabella
Consider him a worthless fellow,

And spurn him with contempt away
Or hear and heed what he would say ?
If he succeed or if he fail,
He will soon to Palos sail.

To know at once what can be done,
He now must take his little son,
Bereft by death of mother's care,
With him, his father's wants to share.

So bidding now his friends adieu,
His journey soon he will pursue,
Then on a vessel bound for Spain,
A passage there at once they gain.

Now when they landed, they were seen
Hastening for the king and queen,
Who were then, as writers say,
About a hundred miles away,

COLUMBUS AT THE COURT OF FERDINAND AND ISABELLA.

At Cordova, near the river,
On the banks of Guadalquiver,
Where the army long before
Had battled with the savage Moor ;

And there for years, in war and strife,
Had struggled for the nation's life—
An unpropitious time to bring
His plans before the queen and king.

Across the fields, like any tramps,
They started for the royal camps,
Hoping at once to find the way
To where the Spanish army lay.

Light in purse, but heavy at heart,
Now wan and hungry they depart ;
About a half a league they went,
Before they reached a stone convent

Where the monks he reverenced dwelt,
And in their lone devotions knelt.
Here he sought a piece of bread,
That his dear boy might now be fed.

A learned prior, unknown before,
Now met them at the convent door ;
A hearty welcome they receive,
And hunger's cravings soon relieve.

When to this priest Columbus told
His schemes so strange, his plans so bold,
He promised that he'd help him bring
Them all before the queen and king.

Now, that he might succeed the better,
He gave an introductory letter
To the chaplain of the queen,
Whom Columbus never'd seen.

Beside all this, this learned one
Provides to educate his son ;
So, when from thence Columbus went,
He left his boy in that convent.

And he became, as others can,
A truly wise and learned man.
Columbus now was quite content,
And onward toward Cordova went,

Where he hoped to meet the wise,
Who would not his plans despise ;
But the war so long in Spain
The royal treasury must gain.

No time or means had they to spend,
To such an expedition send ;
Besides all this, they did not care
Marine disasters now to share.

For seven years he seeks in vain
True recognition here in Spain,
And all his plans attempt to show,
But some said yes, and more said no

But now "this speculative fellow "
Was called to meet Queen Isabella,
Who listened to this earnest man
While he unfolded every plan,

And told her how he came to know
That one might west to India go ;
How he could reach that land of gold,
And all its wealth to her unfold.

But should he sail at her command,
And seek and find some unknown land,
That much he surely would enjoy
To be proclaimed her viceroy ;

And that a tithe would be his due
Of all the wealth that should accrue.
But here the queen responded, " No !
With such demands you cannot go ! "

Columbus had no more to say,
But slowly turned and went away,
Hoping to stand a better chance
Before the royal courts of France.

Now when this man had gone away,
The queen so wished she'd bade him stay !
What would be a loss to Spain,
Another crown, she feared, would gain.

She sent a courier on his track,
To speed in haste and bring him back.
When he again before her stands
She now accedes to his demands,

And tells him soon she'll have on hand
Vessels ready to be manned,
That he may leave the Spanish shore
To seek for land unknown before.

Now all his fears that so annoy
Give way to most exultant joy ;
Like darkness of Egyptian night
Before unclouded noonday light.

Before, a " lunatic " was he,
But now an admiral bound to sea.
What gives the most exultant joy,
He is proclaimed a viceroy.

Before him is the unknown land,
With boats and wealth at his command,
And doubtless souls that must be lost
Without the Saviour and his cross.

Into their dark, beclouded night
He will let shine the gospel light
Until, like sainted ones, above,
They'd know of Jesus and his love.

CHAPTER VI.

THREE VESSELS FITTED AND MANNED.

THREE vessels soon, at his desire,
The " Pinta," " Nina," and " Saint Maria," *
Were fitted out at his command,
Waiting only to be manned.

The " Santa Maria " for this trip
Was to be the admiral's ship ;
The commanders of the others
Were to be the Pinzon brothers,

Noted for their wealth untold,
And for their explorations bold.
Such commanders, brave and true,
Would surely help obtain a crew.

Now he calls for volunteers,
But each in Palos greatly fears
Soon to leave his own dear home,
Across an unknown sea to roam.

It's tempting Providence, they say,
To sail this strange, mysterious way ;
So many things they have to fear
That they dare not volunteer.

* " Santa Maria."

That he might be no more delayed,
A draft at once was quickly made,
And some who did not courage show
Were in this way compelled to go.

A proclamation, too, was made
To free the prison renegade,
And let the criminal go free,
Who in these ships would go to sea.

With all these ways at his command,
The vessels all were quickly manned
With debtors, thieves, and bold brigand,
Who with the true courageous stand.

Such a strange and motley band
Had never sailed from any land ;
That they might be prepared for heaven,
The holy sacrament was given.

And so did all on bended knee
Partake before they went to sea.
It were well could that impart
True repentance to the heart.

As they were ready now to sail,
Their friends drew near them, sad and pale,
With trembling voice and tearful eye ;
How could they say the word good-by !

For when they leave their native shore,
They have no hopes to see them more,
For all of these must have their graves
Beneath the ocean's dark cold waves.

Without a single jest or jeer,
Without a word of praise or cheer,
With broken heart and tearful eye,
They leave them all to dare and die.

And now at last their doleful cries
Before the throne of God arise :
" Oh that our friends from us bereft,
Who now go down to certain death,

" May seek and find thy pardoning grace
Before they meet thee face to face !
Oh that we all at last may stand
United there at thy right hand !"

3

CHAPTER VII.

A DESCRIPTION OF THE VOYAGE ACROSS THE OCEAN.

WITH a crew of just six score,
Now they leave their native shore ;
Before a gentle, steady breeze,
The vessels sped away with ease.

Headed for Canary Isles,
They glide along for many miles,
Until they now can see no more
The mountains of their native shore.

Then they murmur and complain
That they have left the shores of Spain.
Soon by some mysterious slip
One of the rudders they unship,

Doubtless by a coward's hand,
That back she must be towed to land ;
But by her commander's skill
He kept her on her voyage still.

Now when they sailed a thousand miles,
They landed on Canary Isles ;
And while the vessel here stayed,
Another rudder soon was made.

THE EMBARKATION OF COLUMBUS AT PALOS, AUGUST 3, 1492.

At last they leave this island shore,
The unknown waters to explore ;
But soon for fear they cannot sleep,
While tossed upon the mighty deep.

And every league they pushed ahead,
The more they murmur, fear, and dread ;
At length a brilliant meteor flies
On flaming wings across the skies.

How then they feared no tongue can tell,
When it near the vessel fell ;
While white with fear or ghastly pale,
The trade winds filled each flapping sail,

And from a state of painful rest,
It quickly drove them to the west.
Each day increased their discontent
As farther from their homes they went,

Until the closest scrutiny
Alone could save from mutiny ;
But while they thought the matter o'er,
Some seaweed from a distant shore

Near the vessels floated round ;
Upon this mass a crab was found.
Proof, indeed, they thought, at hand,
That they were nearing western land.

And when above they raised their eyes,
Some land-birds winged the distant skies,
And some, as if without a fear,
On weary wings came very near.

It was, indeed, a pleasant sight,
To see them on the vessel light ;
Such little birds, the sailors say,
Could not have come from far away.

Before the sad and farewell scene
A prize was offered by the queen,
For any one in this command
Who first should see the unknown land.

There were no more such fear and dread,
While the sailors looked ahead ;
For on the decks do many stand,
Peering for the unknown land.

At last one on the " Pinta " cries :
" I see the land ! I claim the prize !
Oh, see the cloud-capped mountains rise
Toward the golden sunset skies ! "

Then all the sailors from below
Onto the decks now quickly go ;
And when they think they see the shore,
They shout in triumph more and more :

" Hurrah for this delightful shore !
Hurrah, hurrah, for Commodore !
Hurrah for the brave Pinzons, too !
Hurrah for us—the loyal crew ! "

When silence reigned on that night air,
Columbus bowed his knee in prayer—
" I thank thee for thy guiding hand
That brought us safely near to land.

"Thou most exalted Heavenly King,
All the praise to thee we bring."
Then in song all voices raise
And sing the great Redeemer's praise.

Night let her sable curtains fall,
And darkness settled over all ;
But now the sailors cannot sleep,
Rocked in the cradle of the deep.

At the earliest dawn of day
Onto the decks all make their way,
Expecting very soon to stand
Upon a new discovered land.

But what, indeed, was their surprise,
To see the unobstructed skies,
And not a single foot of land
In any view they could command.

They sail and sail for three days more,
But naught they see of any shore ;
Murmuring now both day and night,
Until Columbus saw a light

Gleaming faintly far away,
What it was he could not say ;
Was it a meteor in the skies,
Or did it from the water rise ?

Was it upon the distant land,
Where now he hoped so soon to stand ?
Another man, in glad surprise,
Saw it, he said, distinctly rise,

As if a torchlight on the land,
Borne up by some unsteady hand.
'Twas ten o'clock that autumn night
When first he saw that distant light.

At two o'clock or not before
A sailor surely sees the shore ;
Just above the sunset skies,
Its features now distinctly rise.

And now at last the cannon's ire,
With thunder sound and breath of fire,
Awakes the finny tribes that sleep
Beneath the waters dark and deep,

And tells to all that understand,
That they have surely seen the land ;
So in a glad, exultant way,
All now await the dawn of day.

LANDING OF COLUMBUS ON SAN SALVADOR

CHAPTER VIII.

THE MORNING SCENES—THE LANDING DESCRIBED.

THE morning dawned so bright and fair,
And fragrance filled the balmy air ;
Upon a lovely shore was seen
The face of nature veiled in green,

While verdant parks and orchards stand
In beauty robed on every hand.
Here flowers of a gorgeous hue
In every lawn and woodland grew ;

And trees unknown to them before
They saw on this delightful shore,
With many tempting kinds of fruit
That any fancy could but suit.

Now their little boats they lower,
And stalwart men take up the oar ;
And soon in ecstasy they stand
Upon this new Edenic land.

'Twas August, fourteen ninety-two,
The day they bade their friends adieu ;
When sixty-seven days had passed
They reached this island shore at last.

As soon as they had landed there,
Columbus bowed his head in prayer,
Thanking the God all should adore
That they had safely reached the shore.

His crew in tears around him stand,
And meekly kiss their leader's hand ;
The most rebellious out at sea
Seem here the meekest now to be.

No penitential words they spare,
That they may of his favors share ;
For in this land before untold
They hope to find great wealth in gold.

Now, in the most impressive manner,
He soon unfurls the Spanish banner,
And in a victor's pride and joy
Proclaims himself the viceroy

Of all the new discovered land
That should be found by his command.
He calls this land, unknown before,
The island of San Salvador.

When they in glittering armor stand
Upon this most delightful land,
The natives, filled with fear and dread,
Into a dense old forest fled.

But when no one did them pursue,
They slowly from the woods withdrew,
And gathered timidly around
Where the Spaniards now are found ;

And here in awe-struck wonder stand
To view this strange, celestial band,
Who, doubtless, now came from above,
Perhaps with messages of love.

The scarlet robes, the royal plumes,
That here Columbus now assumes,
Impressed them more than all the rest
That he was from those regions blest.

The Spaniards looked with glad surprise
Into their dark and friendly eyes.
Such splendid forms, and features, too !
Complexion of a golden hue !

Here Nature's children 'round them stand
Just as they came from Nature's hand ;
They seemed all fitted for the skies,
Trained up in Nature's paradise.

The Spaniard now in barter brings
Some sparkling beads for large gold rings
That native belles, while seeking beaux.
Each wore suspended from her nose.

And this exchange of trinkets bright
Filled every one with great delight ;
The natives to the Spanish brave
A rich collation to them gave

Of all the good things that abound,
Which on this island could be found ;
And such a feast of luscious fruit
Would almost any fancy suit.

They passed a very pleasant day,
So the Spaniards now all say,
Where all regarded each a brother,
And fairly dealt with one another.

CHAPTER IX.

THE NATIVES FURTHER DESCRIBED.

WHAT seemed a wonder, but a truth,
All here retained the bloom of youth ;
The oldest seem so young and fair,
No stooping forms or silvered hair.

The men of age, if such are here,
All in the bloom of life appear ;
Is there not on this new-found shore
A place where beauty fades no more ?

Or have they in this sunny clime
A balm that heals the wounds of time ?
Do not the links of life here sever ?
In youth does man live on forever ?

Or does death on each youthful band.
On every brow, lay his cold hand,
Thus breaking every earthly tie ?
In manhood's prime do all here die ?

Death's sentence passed in olden time
Has reached this fair and sunny clime ;
And all to whom God giveth breath
Do here as elsewhere fall in death.

But to these natives it seems plain
That if man dies he lives again ;
That when the spirit leaves its clay,
Unto the hills it makes its way.

Or to the forests grand and fair,
Departed souls do hasten there ;
Immured in caves where they are led,
There are departed spirits fed.

The doleful winds that sigh and moan
Are but the exile spirits' groan ;
The mountain echoes, Indians said,
Were but the voices of the dead.

The ransomed soul its way soon found,
To the happy hunting ground,
Where each at will, with certain aim,
Is sure to get the choicest game.

Such thoughts of heaven do all inspire,
As best can meet the heart's desire ;
The weary soul that would be blest
May find the haven of its rest.

Unto Columbus and his crew
The natives seem so kind and true !
But see ! these men by nature grand
Hold warlike weapons in each hand.

Upon these persons, scars are found
Of wounds received in battle ground ;
Account they give of warlike bands
Who came marauding through their land.

They tell of islands that of late
Have been by war made desolate,
So on this most enchanted ground,
Angels could not here be found.

CHAPTER X.

COLUMBUS and his motley band
Here viewed at will this lovely land ;
Such scenes of grandeur they behold,
But what they seek is wealth of gold.

They ask, as best they can, by signs,
The natives for the golden mines,
And where the pearls and gems abound,
If any such can here be found.

With many signs and outstretched hands
They point toward the southern lands,
Where the plain, much more the fair,
All rings of gold and bracelets wear.

Where lives, indeed, a chieftain bold,
Who has abundant wealth in gold,
And every other thing he wishes,
Who eats and drinks from golden dishes.

They understood them, too, to say,
That at the north, not far away,
Live nations that in warlike bands
Had often plundered these fair lands.

That these northern warriors bold,
Always returned with wealth of gold,
Such good impressions could not fail
To make them anxious soon to sail.

Most strong, indeed, was that belief
That they'd soon find that noted chief,
And thus by means, if not quite fair,
Obtain what gold he well could spare.

That by delay they may not fail,
They now embark and soon set sail ;
With seven natives they return,
That they the Spaniards' tongue may learn.

That these in turn to them may teach
The grand, mysterious, native speech,
So on the islands of this sea
They all interpreters may be.

With these accessions to their crew,
They sailed the placid waters blue,
Soon an island robed in green
Across the silvery waves is seen.

They near this island large and grand,
Call it Conception when they land,
And view such sights as they before
Had seen upon San Salvador.

Columbus to this new-found race,
A name now gives that all embrace ;
Supposing them on India's shore,
They are called Indians evermore.

In vain he looks for costly rings,
Bracelets of gold, and wealthy kings,
For wealth of storehouse, crib, or barn ;
But little balls of cotton yarn,

And gaudy birds, with plumage rare,
Are all the wealth they have to spare ;
When asked for gold and gems most rare,
They point to southern islands fair—

To lands where people surely bring
Most precious treasures to their king ;
There tons of gold they think, they say,
Not far ahead are stowed away.

CHAPTER XI.

THE VOYAGE TO OTHER ISLANDS—EXPERIENCES WITH INDIANS
WHOM THEY FIND IN THEIR CANOES.

THEY spread their sails and catch the breeze,
And leave this land of flowers and trees—
This isle of luscious fruit untold,
Where naught is found of wealth of gold.

Upon the placid waters blue
There glides an Indian canoe,
Paddled by a lusty band
Of natives from this floral land.

Now they near the vessel's side,
On which they saw an Indian guide.
"Oh, what is that?" a sailor cried;
He hears a splash at "Nina's" side,

And sees a wave roll off so fast,
"Is it a porpoise swimming past?"
Above the wave up comes a head:
"Man overboard!" he loudly said.

"A captive that we brought from shore
When sailing from San Salvador!"
He saw his countrymen afloat
In their little log-hewn boat,

4

And quick as thought he makes a leap
From " Nina's " deck into the deep,
And like a fish darts through the wave,
His life and liberty to save,

And safely reaches that canoe
Now floating on the waters blue.
Their paddles now they quickly ply,
And for the woodland swiftly fly.

But now a boat from " Nina's " crew
Hotly does this band pursue ;
The paddles splash, the oars now beat,
The natives make a safe retreat,

And soon they reach the wave-washed shore,
Flee to the woods, are seen no more.
The Spaniards, beaten in the race,
In deep chagrin give up the chase.

Such fruitless efforts they despise,
So take the Indian boat their prize—
An act unjust ; but none need wonder
That Spanish thieves from Indians plunder.

Another light canoe is seen,
Toward this land of living green ;
All alone, an Indian brave
Comes rocking on the dancing wave,

And soon in all his native pride
He reaches " Saint Maria's " side,
And there beside the ship he stands
With balls of cotton in his hands.

And these he hopes that he may sell
To purchase beads and tinkling bell ;
His charm for toys dispels all fear,
When lo ! at last he comes so near

That two, expert to swim and float,
Jump overboard and seize his boat !
A rope around his waist they slip
And drag him bound onto the ship.

Now like an aspen leaf he stands,
Holding within his trembling hands
The balls of cotton yarn ; in brief,
He offers for his own relief.

Columbus kindly, it is said,
A gorgeous cap puts on his head ;
Puts tinkling hawk bells in his ears,
And bids him now dispel his fears ;

Assures him he is safe from harm,
Puts brilliant bracelets on each arm,
And stands him in his little boat
Again the dancing waves to float.

Gives him the yarn he had before,
Sends him rejoicing to the shore.
The natives here are full of glee
When all his trinkets now they see,

The wondrous story hear him tell
Of all that had to him befell ;
How safe and happy all must be
With those good people on the sea.

From near this land of living green
Another island fair is seen,
Above the waves in grandeur rise
Toward the western golden skies.

They lay their course directly west
For this the fairest and the best,
For here the greedy Spaniards bold
Hope soon to load their ships with gold.

The vessels half the distance make,
When they an Indian overtake
In such a little fragile boat
That naught but skill could keep afloat,

Who for this isle had gone ahead,
That there the news he might all spread,
And tell the natives of that band
Who from the skies came to their land.

Columbus now at his desire
Takes him on the " St. Maria,"
Decks him well with trinkets funny,
Feeds him, too, with wine and honey.

Borne by a gentle, balmy breeze,
The vessel sped away with ease,
Till night her mantle spread at last,
When all the boats their anchors cast

'Mid fragrance wafted from the land ;
Near by a shore supremely grand,
He launches now that light canoe
Upon the waters dark and blue.

With gilded gifts all covered o'er
He sends this Indian brave ashore,
That here the natives on the land
Might greet with joy this coming band.

When here the shore his feet had tread,
The tidings strange were quickly spread ;
At morn a large expectant band
Were seen at daylight on the land.

While all around the waters, too,
There swarmed the Indian canoe,
Whose crews, with joy and native pride,
Approached at once each vessel's side,

Each bringing roots and luscious fruit,
And water pure that could but suit ;
Receiving then some little toy
That filled each childlike heart with joy.

Here sugar, too, and honey sweet,
He gave these natives all to eat,
And soon each one of this command
Was warmly greeted on the land.

The dwellings here were neat, indeed,
Though made of palm-leaves and of reed ;
Graceful in structure and in form,
But damp and chilly in a storm.

Again they search in vain for gold,
But here, as previously, are told
That still the precious golden lore
Is found upon another shore.

Not meeting here his great desire,
He hastens on the " St. Maria,"
And soon this vessel leaves behind her
The pleasant isle of Fernandina,

Still sailing for a richer shore,
On which abounds the precious ore,
Where lives the sovereign, chief, or king,
To whom all wealth the people bring.

Sure " Saomenta " o'er the way
Is such an isle, the natives say.
They land upon this island fair,
But neither king nor gold is there.

Song-birds are here of every hue,
And lovely flowers that sip the dew,
And dancing rills, and crystal lake,
And many things that beauty make—

This isle of purple, green, and yellow,
Called by Columbus, Isabella,
On which a friendly people live,
Could not the precious metal give.

When asked where gold and gems are found,
Reply, on " Cuba " they abound ;
They tell by gestures and by signs
Of precious metal in the mines.

Besides all this they understand
That on this isle are cities grand ;
They understood them, too, to say
That vessels large are in the bay.

CHAPTER XII.

SAILING FOR CUBA—BEAUTIFUL SCENERY—VARIOUS SCENES ON THE
ISLAND.

COLUMBUS now his sails all spread,
To seek his fortune just ahead,
To find this wealthy island fair,
And largely in her riches share.

Soon, on a bright October day,
The grandest scenes before them lay—
A verdant mountain towering high,
Whose summit kissed the blushing sky ;

And valleys all below were seen,
Decked in robes of richest green ;
A lovely stream, a river grand,
Was seen meandering through the land ;

A wave-washed shore of pearly white,
All decked in shells like gems most bright,
While foaming waves were tumbling o'er,
And racing up and down the shore.

Unto this lovely island near,
They sail on crystal water clear ;
Until, in great delight at last,
The ships all here their anchors cast.

An eager band now take the oar
And land upon this gem-decked shore ;
The natives, on the hillsides green,
Amazed by this appalling scene,

Are smitten with the gravest fear,
And quickly fly like frightened deer
To bowers on the mountain side
Where they the most securely hide.

Palm-thatched cabins, neat and clean,
Are all along the river seen ;
But when within they looked around,
No one, at all, could there be found ;

Each one had fled in greatest fear
When ocean's strangers ventured near ;
Not one of all that host was found
To tell where gold and gems abound.

They find no wealth of which to boast,
So westward sail along the coast ;
Now ever peering o'er the land
For domes of cities large and grand.

For now they think, as heretofore,
That they are near fair India's shore ;
That they have reached, or surely can,
The far-famed island of Japan.

He coasts along for three days more,
And sees no end to this vast shore ;
So he and all of his command
Think this is continental land ;

That Cathay's realm, for wealth renowned,
Is near at hand and must be found ;
They beat along, a few days more,
What seemed to all an endless shore.

When all above dark storm-clouds frowned,
While maddened waves dashed all around,
They sail directly from the south
Into a little river's mouth.

When here, protected from the blast,
The vessels all their anchors cast.
Upon these most delightful lands
A group of Indian cabins stands ;

But when they reach the shore ahead
The natives all in terror fled ;
Again Columbus tries to reach
Some trembling natives on the beach,

And for this work he sends ashore
A native of San Salvador ;
When he's in hailing distance near,
He greets them all with words of cheer.

The natives listen on the land,
And seem his words to understand ;
So now he lays aside his oar,
Jumps overboard and swims ashore,

And soon among that group he stands,
Entirely helpless in their hands.
Assured by what he has to say,
They treat him in a friendly way.

What filled Columbus with delight,
Before the gathering shades of night,
Twice eight canoes with native braves,
Beside the ships rocked on the waves.

Again he looks in vain for gold,
But thinks he's by the natives told
That sure an inland city lay
About a hundred miles away—

A city grand, with lofty dome,
There was that noted chieftain's home ;
A journey there they'll undertake,
Acquaintance with that chief they'll make.

He sends an embassy of four—
A native of San Salvador,
An Indian guide of Cuba, too,
A Spaniard and a linguist Jew—

With little trinkets to defray
Expenses met along the way,
And royal gifts with them they bring, ·
For that sovereign, chief, or king.

While there the envoys make this trip,
·Columbus now repairs his ship,
And sends explorers all around
To find where treasures can be found.

CHAPTER XIII.

OTHER DISCOVERIES—A HISTORICAL RIDDLE—THE EXPERIENCE OF
THE ENVOYS—HISTORICAL RIDDLE NO. 2—A SEVERE STORM AT
SEA—THE "PINTA" SEPARATES FROM THE OTHER VESSELS—
VARIOUS SCENES AND EXPERIENCES.

COLUMBUS here a boat now takes,
And up the stream a voyage makes,
Seeking spices that when sold
In Europe's marts would yield them gold.

While looking round he sees a blaze
Into which some Indians gaze ;
A bulbous root he sees them take
From 'neath the ashes where they bake.

This bulb, by white men then first seen,
Is now preserved by Paris green.
Its hidden value, then untold,
Was worth a million tons of gold.

And now please tell me, if you know,
What these roots were and where they grow,
And how this root by them first seen
Is now preserved with Paris green.

The envoys sent out now return,
All gather round, the news to learn ;
They tell how through the wilds they stray
Till, more than thirty miles away,

An Indian hamlet neat and clean,
With fifty houses now is seen.
When they these humble dwellings reach,
The linguist Jew attempts a speech

In all the tongues he can command,
But none of these they understand.
They seem to comprehend much more
The speaker from San Salvador ;

For in wonder most profound,
A thousand natives gather round,
And soon these strangers they embrace,
And rub their hands across each face ;

Inspect the wondrous clothes they wear,
And look them o'er with greatest care,
Seeking to know, as best they can,
The wonders of " the coming man."

While they, their hands upon them laid,
And such a close inspection made,
The intrepid Jew and Spaniard bold
Were vainly searching them for gold.

Here on this isle was found a weed
That was nauseous indeed.
The Spaniards thought it quite a joke
To see this weed the natives smoke,

For when they tried the little trick,
They found, alas ! it made them sick.
But in this thing they would not fail,
So take some with them when they sail.

From day to day a habit grew,
Until this weed they smoke and chew ;
And now all nations, white and black,
Follow so blindly in this track—

Following on without a fear
Where fall its victims every year,
Where slaves of habit ever stay
Without will power to break away.

The fleets that in this harbor lay
Were phantom ships that fade away ;
The wealthy kings and cities grand
Were myths on this delightful land.

Columbus here can find no gold,
Though nature yields her wealth untold ;
Before he leaves this shore he slips
The brightest natives on his ships—

The flower of the Indian race,
Each one with lovely form and face ;
Both brilliant men and maidens young,
That they may learn the Spanish tongue,

So when another trip they make
These trained interpreters they'll take.
Again they hope to cross the sea,
Most useful guides they then will be.

Another island now they seek,
The isle the natives call Babique ;
A wealthy land, they surely say,
Not more than sixty miles away.

So eastward bound they set their sail,
But met a boisterous wind and gale ;
A dreary day and night the fleet
Against the angry billows beat.

Columbus faced about his ship,
To back into the harbor slip ;
He signals so the Pinzons know,
And bids them into harbor go.

Martin Alonzo, it is said,
Still with the " Pinta " pushed ahead,
Now all alone to undertake
His own discoveries to make.

When at the dawn of morning's light,
The " Pinta " still was out of sight,
Columbus, filled with deep disgust
That he this captain cannot trust,

Fears he will hasten back to Spain,
The tidings take, the glory gain ;
So, now in sorrow most intent,
Columbus back to Cuba went,

And sails into a harbor fine,
Called by him Saint Catharine,
Near which a river's mouth was seen,
Upon whose banks were meadows green,

Decked with flowers of every hue,
Near which the mammoth oak tree grew,
Canoes of which the Indians make,
That will a hundred persons take.

Columbus is perplexed to know
Where he shall sail, when he shall go,
But soon decides again to seek
The wealthy isle they call Barbique.

Doubting, fearing, lest they fail,
From Cuba's eastern point they sail;
Soon mountains decked in robes of green
A little south of east were seen.

But when this land the Indians spied,
All on the ships were terrified;
" It is the Caribs' isle," they cry,
" Who torture prisoners till they die;

"And all who come within their power
They surely kill and then devour."
And then in tears they all implore
That none will land on that dark shore.

Columbus fearing naught they said,
Toward this island pushed ahead—
Toward fair Hayti's western shore,
Just as he had done before.

Armed and equipped at great expense,
Could he not stand in self-defence ?
Why need he fear these fiends so bold,
If that fair land abounds in gold ?

They near these towering mountains high,
Whose summits pierce the vaulted sky,
And looking all around he sees
The most luxuriant forest trees.

Through towering pine and sturdy oak,
He sees arise a cloud of smoke;
So all of this opinion share,
That crowds of men are gathered there.

Over the billows on they glide,
And in a pleasant harbor ride,
And soon a lovely shore they reach,
Canoes they find upon the beach.

Deserted villages are seen
On hillside slopes and all between;
But here they seek in vain to find
A single native left behind.

Attempts to reach the natives fail,
So they embark and eastward sail;
Saint Nicholas Harbor leave behind,
For Port Conception now to find.

They soon this pleasant harbor reach,
And land upon a pearly beach;
But here the frightened natives fly
To clefts upon the mountain high.

Armed men are sent out, but in vain,
To access to the people gain.
A wandering band with nimble feet
Now chanced some islanders to meet.

As soon as these the natives spied,
They all were greatly terrified ;
And for the mountains off they bound
Like frightened deer before a hound.

And here a lovely Indian maid,
Who with this native band had strayed,
Now seeks in vain to keep apace
With other runners in the race,

With her trained brothers all so fleet.
In their precipitous retreat
The sailors, weary in the race,
Would soon have given up the chase;

But when they saw her faltering step,
Onward for victory they kept ;
And soon their shouts of triumph rise,
As with their fascinating prize

They quickly to the vessel go,
And proudly here their prize now show.
A ring of gold hung from her nose,
Which led Columbus to suppose

That this treasure could be found
In abundance all around.
Columbus greets this maiden fair,
As with parental love and care.

The Indian belles from Cuba here
Assurance give, dispel her fear;
And then her person they adorn,
Like ruddy sky at blushing morn,

With gaudy robes so fair and bright,
That thrilled her with intense delight;
They decked her now with trinkets funny,
And gave her, too, both wine and honey.

5

So when at last they bade her go,
She seemed inclined to answer No.
Some sailors now with boat and oar
So slowly set this belle ashore.

Then all alone they let her stray
To her own village far away,
That here her story she may tell,
And all her brothers' fears dispel.

The morning dawned—a band of ten
Most bold, impetuous, daring men,
Who never think of saying fail,
Followed in an Indian trail

Through the forests where had strayed
That most attractive Indian maid.
When near a river winding round
A thousand wigwams there they found ;

But when these warriors came so near
The natives fled in greatest fear,
For the adorning of the maid
Had doubtless made them more afraid.

They seemed instinctively to know
That there approached a wily foe,
Who would delusive means employ,
So sent them now this fair decoy.

A Cuban guide, most loyal shown,
Pursued these natives all alone ;
And soon he gains the listening ear—
His words at once dispel their fear.

Two thousand natives (it seems queer)
Now gathered round without a fear ;
And with the ten they make a trip
Back to Columbus and the ship.

They dazzle now the natives' eyes
With gaudy trinkets that surprise,
And now some little presents make,
And so, of course, some presents take.

Some brilliant beads each Spaniard brings
And freely gives for large gold rings ;
A little gold the sailors find
That they would not leave behind.

CHAPTER XIV.

EXPERIENCE WITH AN INDIAN CHIEF—LOSS OF THE " SANTA
MARIA "—THE RETURNING VOYAGE.

To make a lengthy story brief,
They found at last an Indian chief,
Kind-hearted, generous, and true.
With whom the warmest friendship grew.

And every courtesy then known
Was by and to that chieftain shown ;
Columbus made a great parade,
And just the same that chieftain made.

Columbus with him went to dine,
And with him freely drank his wine ;
Delightful games the Spaniards play
With these kind natives while they stay.

Such pleasures very soon are passed,
Or with them sorrow comes at last ;
One very fair and pleasant night,
When from the shore, not out of sight,

The " Santa Maria," so they say,
Within a pleasant harbor lay ;
All are surprised when it is found
That she has surely run aground,

And every effort that is sought
To make her float avails them naught.
Columbus and his crew now know
That she must soon to pieces go.

At morn Columbus sought relief
From Guacanagari the chief,
Who mourned their lot and freely wept,
And very helpful to them kept.

He sends to aid brave men and true,
Each native with his own canoe ;
Those little boats with goods were stored,
Until the ship they all unload.

So crew and cargo now all land
Safely with this native band,
And here protected find relief
With this kind-hearted Indian chief.

Here all the help that he could render,
His kind heart prompted him to tender ;
The " Santa Maria " none could save,
She went to pieces on the wave.

Now on this shore a fort they make,
In which her ordnances they take,
And on this fair and fruitful ground
Attempt a colony to found.

And here they leave some forty men,
To what they leave behind defend,
And with much care to look around
To find where gold and gems abound.

And now Columbus and his crew
Bid all they leave behind adieu,
And on the " Nina," small and frail,
Prepare, at once, to homeward sail.   `

When leaving this delightful sea,
They find the savage Caribbee;
The real Cannibal they meet,
Who surely kill, and kill to eat.

But here these Indians found it vain
To fight these warriors late from Spain,
And soon they made a quick retreat,
Hungering still, with naught to eat.

Now all aboard the ship again,
They weigh their anchor, sail for Spain;
What filled each one with great delight,
The " Pinta " here heaves up in sight,

That all alone had cruised around,
And many things delightful found.
And so the two move off together
'Mid boisterous waves and stormy weather.

For days and weeks a howling blast
Fearfully shook each trembling mast !
But here the tempest wild and grand
Was in our loving Father's hand,

Whom much Columbus did implore,
To bring them safely back to shore;
So all at last in triumph stand
Upon their own dear native land.

A message to the king was sent,
The tidings through all Europe went,
And such a glad, exultant day
Was never known, so writers say.

The drums all beat, the cymbals clang,
The bells from every steeple rang,
Crowned heads arise upon their feet,
The greatest man in Spain to greet.

And every one desires to be
With him who crossed the unknown sea.
Four hundred years have passed away,
Since that most glad, triumphant day.

But since that time so long ago,
Some changes have been made, you know;
But what they are you all know well
That pen and tongue can never tell.

www.ingramcontent.com/pod-product-compliance
Lightning Source LLC
Chambersburg PA
CBHW032358020726
47499CB00008B/2812